COPYRIGHT © 2021 BY ROFHIWA COLLINS MULOVHEDZI

Ordering information: To place your order send an email at crofhiwa66@gmail.com, the book also available on Amazon.

All scripture quotation are from the New Living Translation 2013

☐

Printed by:
Company Name

Printed in South Africa

First Printing Edition, 2021
ISBN 978-0-620-94007-8

The character and Acts of a Reformed Heart

Christianity lies in the Heart

TABLE OF CONTENTS

ABOUT THE BOOK

The book The Character and Acts of a reformed Heart is an effective weapon that teaches Christians who are living in these end times how to maintain a relationship with God and fully operate in the spirit by guarding their hearts during these troubling times. The book shows how Christians can open up their hearts and their spirit as their God is spirit and those who worship him must do so in spirit. This is a mind-challenging, life-changing and spiritual transforming book based on the very living word of God.

FOREWORD

Christianity is not a religion but an everyday lifestyle, it is not something we only do on a special occasion or in happy times only but our everyday living. In Christianity we carry the cross and run the race, we endure through tough times, we praise God in good and bad times making sure that our hearts remain pure and free because Christianity lies in the heart. God does not judge a man by the color of his skin, influence you have or position that you have in life, God looks at the contents of your heart and it is only when you seek him with a free heart that you will find him.

WHAT IS A REFORMED HEART?

A reformed heart, a free heart, by heart I mean the inner man, the breath that God breathed into the clay. A free heart, this phrase is made up of two words (free and heart). Free comes from the word freedom which is defined as the state of being free, of not being imprisoned or enslaved. In this book, we are referring this phrase to spiritual freedom, a free heart, not enslaved, and a heart that is not bonded or under any kind of York. The bible say that where the spirit of God is there is freedom, and God lives in us, so we must be free.

Now medically the heart is the most important organ in the human body because it holds life in such a way that if it stops operating the whole body dies. The function of the heart in the human body is to transport blood to the rest of the body, if there is a problem with the heart the whole body will also have a problem and will suffer. The heart transports things throughout the body so that the whole system of the body can function. For example take the heart as an engine of a car and the car as the human body, if there is no engine the car cannot move or function and if the engine has problems the car will have problems.

Here am talking about the inner heart, the inner heart or soul. Man has two natures, the physical nature and the spiritual nature, the physical nature is the one you can see with the naked eye and consist of the body, organs such as the heart and brain (these are the most important one). The Physical nature operates through the five senses which are sight, taste, touch, smell and hearing. The physical nature is a mirror image of the spiritual nature, it resembles the spiritual nature, which is the foundation of life, because life is in the spirit, to understand this concept more get my other book *life in the spirit.* All forces holding and controlling life are in the spirit. The spiritual nature consists of the spirit which is the body of the spiritual nature and the soul which is the heart of the spiritual nature, lastly the mind which is the brain of the spirit. Now same as in the physical nature if the heart (organ) is affected the whole body and system is affected, also in the spiritual nature if the heart soul) is affected the whole spiritual nature is affected because from the soul (inner heart) is where feeling, emotions and thoughts

12

originate and procced. When I talk about the heart in this book am referring to the inner heart the soul of the spirit. Now as a child of God and as a Christians you must have free hearts to be able to function in the nature that God wants you to be. You see the heart is the most important thing, your spiritual heart I mean, yes the very same heart you love with, hate with and through which feeling overflow from.

Proverbs 4:23

Guard your heart above all else, for it determines the course of your life.

A free heart is a heart that is not burdened by anything, not heavy, nothing prohibiting or preventing it to be able to function (to do its job in a Christian life). A free heart is free from things of this World, it is not bound or chained by anything, and it is an overcoming heart.

WHY A FREE HEART

1 Samuel 16:6-7

But the Lord said to Samuel don't judge by his appearance or height, for I have rejected him. The Lord does not see things the way you see them. People judges by the outward appearance, but the Lord looks at the heart.

Something that we must realize as Christians is that our God is a God who works or operates through the heart. The heart is the most important part of a Christian life. First of all your salvation would not be complete or be possible without the heart for it is by the heart that you believed and you were saved. It is the spirit that gets saved not the flesh (organs) but the inner heart/soul and mind that are transformed.

Romans 10:9-10

If you openly declare that Jesus is Lord and believe in your heart that God raised him from the dead, you will be saved. For it is by believing in your heart that you are made right with God, and by openly declaring your faith that you are saved.

You see it all start in the heart for God works through the heart, whatever God wants to do to any person a Christian or not the father in heaven first looks at the heart of that person, he looks at what is inside the heart of that person. A person is not the outside appearance that we see but the heart defines who a person is.

As we are living in this world we come across many challenges and trials, especially in these last days we are living in, days spoken about in the bible, days prophesied by the prophets of the most high God.

As a Christian you need a free heart to be able to serve God, you cannot serve God if your hearts is not free.

Deuteronomy 10:12

And now, Israel, what does the Lord your God require of you? He requires only that you fear the Lord your God, and live in a way that pleases him, and love him and serve him with all your heart and soul.

You need your hearts to be free for you to be able to serve God and fully operate in His nature. One thing that many Christians don't realize and that which must be taken into consideration is that the trials and challenges you come across are not meant to destroy you or to take you down but to take you to another level. Challenges, trials and tests are things which God use to prepare you to the next level which God want you to be in, often we run from the very things that will strengthen our lives, such as trials, temptation and pains of various kind.

Yes, the challenges may seem like they are not bringing any good in your life, but God just allows them to happen for a reason, it might be to bring you close to him, it might be to preserve you, and it might be to make your faith strong but never to destroy you. In the previous sentence, I said God allows the challenges and trials we face to happen, yes He does allow them to happen not that He is the one causing them to happen but it's the devil, remember the story of Job which we will talk about later. Everything bad that happens in our lives the cause of it is the devil, the word of God said he came to steal kill and destroy and that's his work that he is doing. Our adversary the devil does all these things with a purpose and his purpose is to take you out from God, it is to stop your heart from loving God. You will agree with me when you came across bad things in life the heart is the one that is affected, it is the one that gets tired and it is the one that gets discouraged because in a human all things have to do with the heart. Now he does all these things to attack the heart and to remove your heart from God and believing in him and his words. The devil himself knows that if your heart is troubled you cannot be able to serve God.

Jesus Christ our Lord also knew this, He knew that our hearts must be free so that we can be able to do the work He left for us to finish here on earth, and He knew that the enemy will test us and that we will face many things that will trouble our hearts and our spirits. That's why He said to his disciples in the book of John that they should not let their hearts be troubled for His peace is with them.

John 14:27

I am leaving you with a gift-peace of mind and heart. And the peace I give is a gift the world cannot give. So don't be troubled or afraid.

If your heart is troubled nothing good will come out of you and you will not be able to complete the assignment in your life that He has called you for. An anxious heart weighs a man down and that man will not be able to bear fruits.

As I have said in the last part that your enemy (devil) also knows of this, that if your heart is troubled you cannot be able to serve God. Remember he once lived in the presence of God so he knows how God operates.

In the story of Job, the word of God said one day the assembly of God was meeting and the devil availed himself, God said to him did you saw my servant Job how faithful he is then the adversary said it is because you do good things for him only, do bad things and you will see he will never worship you, as I have said because God is not the cause of bad things he allowed the devil to bring bad things into Jobs life.

God gave Job into the hands of the devil to do anything to him and his family, mind you while the devil was afflicting Job he aimed to trouble Jobs' hearts and stop him from worshipping God. He attacked him through, sickness, disappointment, discouragement and affliction. This is what the devil do us Christians he brings all sort of bad things to trouble us and to make us stop worshipping God in so doing losing our salvation and fellowship with God. That's why we must not worry or grumble when we came across bad things but rather rejoice because we know that we are being prepared for another level.

James 1:2

Dear brothers and sisters, when troubles of any kind come your way, consider it an opportunity for great joy.

The amount of trials and challenges you face in life determines the kind of destiny you have, in other words, how big your destiny is, is defined by the trials and challenges you face today. The bigger the test the bigger the reward.

The revelation here is that trials most of the time come when God is about to bless us, I believe that when God gathered with his assembly He was about to bless Job but the adversary accuse him because he is our accuser and brought about all the bad things in Jobs life.

All this the devil did to trouble Job's heart and move it away from God, the devil knew that if Jobs hearts its troubled he will Miss God's blessing. All these things that were happening to Job caused him pain, his children were killed, he lost all his wealth, he was sick to the point of death, but Job never allowed his heart to be troubled, even when his friend encouraged him to just curse God and die, he remained in faith and his heart was not moved. He knew that whether things are good or bad God is still God.

The problem with many Christians today is that we allow our hearts to be troubled and that's what Satan wants, for your hearts to be troubled so that you cannot be able, to pray, praise God and just to stop us from serving God. He brings things, situations and challenges which attack your heart and faith.

The sickness that you have as a child of God is not meant to kill you but is a test of faith, we will talk about tests in the next chapter. A test is to see if you can be moved from the faith by circumstance. That's why it is so important that you do not allow your hearts to be troubled by such things but rather they should make you strong in faith, in the father and spirit.

Many things happen in our lives, as we are living In this earth as children of God we are at war, we are fighting for our faith, for our salvation. Jesus Christ said in the book of **John 16:33** " here on earth you will have many trials and sorrows. But take heart I have overcome the world".

So Christ has overcome, and he has also overcome for you, you do not have to worry about anything. No matter what happens in your life you must stand and not let your heart be troubled, for all things are working together for good for you. It doesn't mean that when you are a Christian you won't come across situation or challenges, no you are bound to come across them so the power of God can be seen. Never make the mistake of judging your Christianity by the circumstance of your life, falling in life, coming across disappointments and being poor does not mean you are not a true Christian, Christianity lies in the heart. Remember the story of Lazarus and the rich man. And never make the mistake of judging your Christian life by the success you have, life is not in material things but in the spirit.

There are many people, many Christians who should be far in life, far in the things of God, servant of God who should be doing great things in the kingdom of God, but nothing is happening because their hearts are not free. Many people should be serving God, but their hearts are hindering the purpose of God in their lives. Remember the story of David when the Lord wanted to choose a new king for his people, He said to the prophet Samuel I am sending you to Jesse of Bethlehem, I have chosen one of his sons to be king of Israel. When Samuel arrived he saw Eliab and thought he is the one because of his appearance and body stature. But God said is not him, I do not look at the outward appearance but I look at the heart.

God does not look at your outward appearance, how rich you are, how poor you are, how hard you pray but He looks at your heart, whether you have the heart of God or not. Some people God want to bless and some to use but when he looks at their hearts He is not pleased. Our hearts must be free and be pleasing to God.

You need to release your heart from bondage, you must release your heart from the pain of the past, from hatred. You need to release yourself so that you can have freedom. Don't hold yourself self-hostage, don't imprison yourself by holding offence and grudges. For God to bless and release you, you must first release yourself and free your heart.

Many of us have been through a lot, have been hurt by people we loved, people who we never expected could hurt us and that have left a wound in our hearts that pains us and torment us. You have to release yourself so that your heart can be free because if your heart is not free it will hold you back in life from moving forward. You are the only one who can release yourself by forgiving (forgiveness).

Faith is
Of
Man's
heart

FAITH

Now what is faith and what does it have to do with a free heart. Faith the word of God in the book of Hebrews says

Hebrews 11: 1

Faith is the confidence that what we hope for will happen, it gives us assurance about things we cannot see.

Faith is the substance of things hoped for, the evidence of things not yet seen, and faith is not touchable but it is a spiritual thing. I define faith as a divine spiritual force, anointing that causes something to happen, it forces things from the spirit to manifest physical where everyone can see them. So faith is a spiritual thing as I have said and we cannot talk about the spiritual things without the heart because your heart is the one that connects you with the spiritual realm.

To be able to express or excise faith you need a free heart, some people say I have faith but they don't see the result of the faith they say they have because faith must bear fruit or must produce the result, and every time you applying something and not working it means there is something you doing wrong, I say to you faith without a free and pure heart is ineffective. The word of God and all scriptures will never come to pass in your life if your heart is not free and pure, you can quote all the scriptures but without a free heart, there will be no result. " a good man brings good things out of the good stored up in his heart, and an evil man brings the evil stored up in his heart". A free heart is a key to make your faith effective and to have the result.

A free heart is also essential for the battle we are fighting, the book of Ephesians says we are not wrestling against flesh and blood but against spiritual host of wickedness in the heavenly places, therefore to be victorious we must also fight in spirit and for that, we need a free heart and a pure heart that can operate in the spirit and excise faith, the faith which comes from the heart. Mind you true faith, faith that is effective comes from a pure heart, a free heart.

A heart that is not free, that is burdened, enslaved will not be able to excise true faith and operate in true faith that a child of God must operate in and that is great faith. There are two types of faith, namely, the faith that everyone receives when they accept Jesus Christ, the **little faith** and the most effective one and needed one is **great faith**. Everyone received a measure of faith from God and is your duty to grow that faith.

LITTLE FAITH

This kind of faith is the poor faith that no child of God must not dwell in as it does not accomplish or get the work done, it may start it but it is unable to complete the work. Jesus does not want or likes us to have this kind of faith. We see this in the book of Matthews where the disciples of Jesus got into the boat and sallied without him, in the middle of the night they saw him walking on the top of the water, Peter asked to come to him also walking on top of the water.

When Peter started walking on top of the water the waves rose and was coming to him and fear entered him and he started sinking. Jesus saved him and after He said you of little faith why doubt. This kind of faith is not good because it starts the work but when things heat up it produces fear and doubt and in the end, it fails.

We do not need this kind of faith that is unable to be patient and persevere, which when situations start to get worse it starts to weaver and we fear that whether we will make it or not. Yes, it is faith but it is not complete faith and won't produce the result. Peter's heart was distracted, it went from being free to be invaded by fear and it affected his faith and that caused him not to reach his goal to where Jesus was.

A heart that is not free, a heart that is full of fear, hatred, complaints, jealousy, greedy and grudges will affect your faith and will lead you to failure.

GREAT FAITH

This is the kind of faith that as children of God we must operate in. For it is the faith that gets the work done, the faith that accomplishes the task. It is the faith that does not look at the situation at hand, faith that does not waver no matter the circumstances and most importantly the faith that Christ wants us to have.

Matthew 8:5-10.

The scripture above is about Jesus and the centurion, according to the scripture when Jesus came into Capernaum a centurion whose servant was sick came to Jesus crying that

Jesus should heal his servant that he had left home. Jesus agreed to go with him to his servant but the centurion said to Jesus, Lord just say a word and my servant will be healed. Jesus hearing this was very pleased and said verily I tell you I have not found so great faith, not in Israel.

This man excised such great faith and by which the servant was healed same time without Jesus going with him to the sick servant. This kind of faith can only be achieved by a free heart, the faith that does not say tomorrow, next week or next year but it says this instance it is done. It is only a free heart that can be able to declare the impossible possible. When the bible said you shall declare a thing and it shall come to pass, it was referring using this kind of faith, faith that moves mountains, faith that says am healed when doctors are saying you are sick and will die, faith that conquers and gets the scriptures to be fulfilled in our lives.

Faith is important to us as Christians, more especially the great faith. Take faith as the currency of heaven that with it you are able to purchase heavenly things like healing, breakthrough, deliverance and miracles. The more faith you have the more heavenly goods you will be able to purchase. All this can be allocated to those who have faith, remember faith only can please God. You can grow your faith by hearing and reading more of God's word, the more you know about God the more your faith will increase because faith comes by hearing and hearing of the word of God.

NOT FEARFUL

A free heart is not a place of fear, it is a place of peace, and it is a place of joy. Jesus said in the book of John "whoever believes in me out of his heart shall flow rivers of living water" meaning the Holy Spirit. A free heart is not a place of doubt that can be easily shaken by challenges. You are living in fear every day because your heart is not free from worries.

A free heart has a clear consciousness, when we say a person has conscious we mean that the person is aware and sensitive to observing and noticing or being strongly interested or concerned about something.

Your consciousness is a tool that God uses to search your heart through the Holy Spirit. A free conscious means a free heart, many people today live in fear because their consciousness is not free and your consciousness is one thing that will never lie to you. Our conscious judges us before God himself judges us, a free conscious means you are convicted of yourself, you are sure of yourself. If your consciousness is free you won't live in fear, fear of failing, fear of death or fear of sickness.

Many of us are living in fear because we know through our consciousness that our hearts are not right with God, we doubt ourselves, and where there is doubt there is fear.

For Paul to be able to say for me to live is Christ and to die is to gain it is because his heart was free and his conscience was clear, he was sure of his standing with Christ. It is very important as a Christian to have a clear conscience, once you're conscious is clear you will never have fear but will live confidently in Christ.

PRAYERFUL

Prayer is a spiritual language that everyone who calls themselves a Christian must speak every day as long as they are still on this earth, a Christian will not be able to function or won't be complete without prayer. Prayer is of the heart, it is a thing of the heart then it manifest by actions but it actually starts in the heart. Many of the times your prayers are not answered because your heart is not free and if your heart is not free it means your prayer was not from the heart but you were only showing the action of prayer, or your prayer was from the heart, but what kind of heart? Is it pleasing to God? A prayer coming from a place where there is no peace, full of unforgiveness and not pure can never be effective.

A heart that is not free grieves the Holy Spirit which will result in you not being able to function in spirit, your prayer will just become words without meaning and authority. Prayer is a spiritual thing and we cannot speak about the spirit without involving the heart, the heart of a Christian is a door into the spiritual realm through the Holy Spirit. Our Lord Jesus was a person of prayer, the bible says he would often withdraw himself from his disciples to go and pray, he was able to do this because his heart was free, he was not grieving the holy spirit. When your heart is free and Holy Spirit is not grieved, Holy Spirit will tell you and led you to pray, he will give you the strength to pray and it will no longer be you who is praying but the holy spirit in you will be the one praying. You cannot be able to pray if your heart is not free.

An affected heart, a grieved spirit, an injured spirit cannot be able to reach and touch God, that is you need a free heart to pray. A heart that is free is free from things of this world, free from its surrounding and it's not affected by what happens around it.

Roman 12:12.

Rejoice in our confident hope. Be patient in trouble and keep on praying.

The statement keep on praying in other words be faithful in prayer shows that there are things that will come and try to render us useless in prayer, but it is only those whose hearts are free that can remain faithful in prayer because they no longer pray on their own but through the holy spirit. Prayer is not just the word we speak but the heart and the spirit must also be in prayer agreeing with the words that we are speaking.

Ephesians 6:18.

Pray in the spirit at all times and on every occasion....

This scripture shows us that it is possible for one to pray in the flesh which is wrong and bad and it can be caused by having a heart that is not free. People who pray in the flesh their prayers are based on feeling, on what people are saying and by what is happening in their lives, these people end up praying prayers that are out of Gods will. A Christian should and must always pray in the spirit, in so doing your prayer will be effective because the spirit will bring revelation about

what you have to pray for and how to
pray.

TEST OF FAITH

The devil testing Jesus

The bible in the book of Luke chapter 4 shows that after Jesus was tested by the devil and had conquered all the tests of the devil, He returned filled with the power of the Holy Spirit, filled with the anointing of God. He was no longer the same way he was before he went to the desert to be tested.

Something great had happened to him, and that was caused by the test and him conquering the test, these were the words of Jesus after coming back from the wilderness...

Luke 4 verse 18

The spirit of the Lord is upon me, for he has anointed me to bring Good news to the poor. He has sent me to proclaim that captives will be released, that the blind will see, that the oppressed will be set free, and that the time of the lord favor has come.

As children of God we are bound to come across trials and challenges, it is very impossible that as long as we are living on this earth we are not tested, but the tests that come our way are meant for our promotion, they are there to take us to another level. Test are there to prepare us for our assignment in life, tests make us seek God more for it is when we are facing challenges that we will pray more, they also make us be dependent on God and know that without him we cannot do anything.

Without test in our Christian life, we would remain in the same position, our faith would not grow and we would stay in the same place and we won't grow spiritually. So tests are very important in a Christian's life because they move us forward, we must not complain or feel discouraged when we face tests but rather rejoice and be patient.

WHAT TO DO WHEN FACING TRIALS

Exodus 14:10-11.

As Pharaoh approached, the people of Israel looked up and panicked when they saw the Egyptians overtaking them. They cried out to the Lord, and they said to Moses, why did you bring us out here to die in the wilderness? Weren't there enough graves for us In Egypt? What have you done to us? Why did you make us leave Egypt?

The scripture above is a very common one, this was after pharaoh the Egyptian king allowed to release the

Israelites and set them free to go and worship their God under the leadership of Moses, the people of God were encamped near Pi-Hahiroth close to the red sea.

The Egyptian then came after them, when the Israelites looked back they saw the Egyptians coming after them, when they looked in front the Red sea was standing before them, the Israelites were trapped, fear invaded them, they panicked and started complaining to Moses the servant of God. The Israelites had lost all hope and faith at this point, they have forgotten all that the Lord has done for them, all the miracles he performed in their midst.

This is what most of us Christians do when we come across challenges and test, we forget what the Lord has done for us in the past, we forget that he is the one who brought us where we are today. By doing that we end up being defeated by the challenges, we end up falling the test. This is not how we are supposed to act or react when we face trials and challenges.

Daniel 3:16-18

Shadrach, Meschach and Abednego replied "o Nebuchadnezzar, we do not need to defend ourselves before you. If we are thrown into the blazing furnace, the God whom we serve is able to save us, he will rescue us from your power, your majesty. But even if he doesn't, we want to make it clear to you, your majesty, that we will never serve your gods or worship the gold statue you have set up.

Here we hear about the three men of God who in the land that they were staying in the king made an image of God and commanded all the people of

62

the land to worship the image of gold.
This became a problem to these men
because worshipping an image made by
human hands was against their faith,
this was against what they believed in
and it was a challenge to them, a test of
faith because the king said whoever
that does not worship the image of gold
will be thrown into the fire.

These men were not shaken or moved
by this but stood their ground and said
no we will not worship the image for we
know our God, they said our God will
rescue us, listen to this, they said even
if he does not rescue us we will not
worship your gods. Now that's

powerful, these men knew and understood that God is God no matter what, they knew that whether things are good or bad God remains God. We must not praise God only when He does good things in our lives, God is still God even when there are bad things happening.

Whether we die or live that does not change the fact that God is God, He existed before creation, and He is God by nature and by His own will. This is how you must be in your mind and heart, and this is how you must be in your mind as a Christian when you come across challenges.

You must stand your ground and not allow to be moved by circumstances. You must fully trust in the Lord and know that He will never forsake you for He is always with you and you have an assurance for that and the assurance is Jesus Christ. The bible says in **Matthew 1 verse 23** "Behold a virgin shall give birth to a child and they shall call him Emmanuel, which means God is with us.

Beloved God is with you and He is always with you, so no need to worry and complain when we are tested, He said when you pass through the water He will be with you, when you pass through the rives He will be with you, they shall not overflow you and when you walk through the fire you shall not be burned, nor shall the flame scorch you. All you have to do is believe in Him and his words, for God knows the plans He has for you, plans not to harm you but to prosper you.

Acts 16:25

Around midnight Paul and Silas were praying and singing hymns to God.....

The scripture above is about when Paul and Silas were in prison, beaten, chained and in pain. They were in a very serious predicament, but these men did not look at how badly they were beaten, they did not listen to the pain they were feeling, but they praised God, yes they praised God, they did not cry onto the Lord to ask him to rescue them, but they praised him it that difficult situation they were in. This teaches us that when we face test and challenges what we have to do is to praise God, praising God releases the anointing to set you free. In the midst of challenges and test what you have to do is stand your ground and praise God without stopping believing in him.

GOD'S TIME IS THE BEST

Time, the indefinite continued progress of existence and events in the past, present and the future. We are living in a universe where everything is controlled by time. As the bible say's in the book of Ecclesiastes that under heaven there is a season and time for every activity.

Yes, your life here on earth is controlled by God who is in control of time and as a Christian, your life is in God's hands and whatever that must happen or that you desire to happen in your life will happen only in God's time. Sometimes you want things to happen in your lives in a certain way and at a certain time, you pray and fast for those things to happen and they don't, does it mean God did not hear you? no, not all. What you must know as a Christian is that there is the time of man and there is a time of God. It is very important that we know and understand time and seasons in our life's so that we might know Gods will in doing so our heart won't be troubled and we won't be discouraged.

Many are the plans in a man's heart but is the Lord's will that prevails. God's time is the best because God is the creator of everything and He knows what is best for you and when it will be best for you to get what you want. You may want something so desperately that you pour your heart out to God, but don't get it just because to him is not the right time for you to get what you want.

Yes to you it might seem like it is the right time but you must remember that the way you think and see things is not the same as the Lord's.

Isaiah 55:8

"My thoughts are nothing like your thoughts," says the Lord.

"And my ways are far beyond anything you could imagine".

So when you are not getting what you desire or what you are praying for, you don't have to give up, it does not mean God doesn't want to answer you or He does not hear you, but it just means that it is not yet God's perfect time for you to receive what you want, we have so many Christians that prayed for something for so many years and got those things after a long time when they have even forgotten that they prayed for such things.

What you have to do as a child of God when you pray for something and there seems to be no change is to be still and know that God will surely fulfil his promise. "For all the promise of God in him are yes, and in Him Amen, to the glory of God through us. Do not mistake God's patience for his absence, his timing is perfect, and his presence is constant, he is always with you, for he is omnipresent.

HOW TO HEAL A DAMAGED HEART

Things do happen in life, challenges come, tribulation comes, persecution and disappointment. All of these things we are bound to come across in our life, we were born into this world of suffering and sin, yet we are just passing by and the only way to be saved is through Jesus Christ.

ACTS 4:12

There is salvation in no one else! God has given no other name under heaven by which we must be saved

The first step to take to heal a hurt heart is to forgive, if you really want to free your heart you must forgive, forgive all the people who have wronged you, forgive those who have hurt you and disappointed you. No matter what they did, forgive. That's the first step to living a life of peace and freedom. Forgive yourself also for the mistakes and things you have done that you are not proud of. This is the only way to release your heart and inviting God and the Holy Spirit to intervene and to the work of comforting.

Matthew 18:21-22

Then Peter came to him and asked, "Lord, how often should I forgive someone who sins against me?

Seven times? No, not seven times. Jesus replied, "But seventy times seven.

Here Jesus was showing us how important it is to forgive. Forgiving means you leave everything onto God's hands, you take your pain to him and he will give you comfort and the joy of the Lord becomes your strength.

Matthew 11:28-30.

Then Jesus said, "come to me, all of you who are weary and carry heavy burdens, and I will give you rest. Take my yoke upon you. Let me teach you because I am humble and gentle at heart, and you will find rest for your souls. For my yoke is

easy to bear, and the burden I give you is light.

You may have been hurt by your loved ones, people you least expected to hurt you, for us to be able to live a free life of freedom and peace we must forgive and give everything to Christ.

It is only Christ that can heal the heart, no doctor, no medicine that can heal a broken hurt or an injured spirit, only Christ the creator of the heart can heal it. That's why he said come to me all who are weary, I will heal you and you will find rest for your souls.

Another thing to do is to focus on God and yourself. You have to stop focusing on other people and focus on your life and your God. The more time you spend focusing on other people the more your life is falling apart. Many people get hurt because they are so much focused on other people's lives and forget about their own. Never compare your life with that of a fellow brother or sister because we are different. Everyone here on earth came alone and will also leave alone, we all have different purposes which God has destined for us. Find your purpose and focus on it and on God, then you will live a victorious life.

Lastly, forget the past, do not dwell on the past because you can never change the past, but you can only learn from it.

Focus on the future because you can change the future, the Lord said in the book of the prophet Isaiah "behold am doing new things" so do not dwell on the past because by doing so you prevent God from doing new things in your life. Do not dwell on those failures, on that pain of the past and on that disappointment but focus on God.

YOUR VISION

Vision can be defined in so many ways, a vision can be that of a dream or that of a trance. Vision, in this case, we can say is the manifestation to the senses of something immaterial, in simple terms it is seeing the future while you are in the present. Vision shows you where you are going. Poor is the man without vision, vision is revealed truth that is divine, that is from God. As Christians, we have one and only vision in common and that is to see the kingdom of heaven. Yes, the vision of every Christian must be to enter heaven, you are already granted entrance into the kingdom when you repented and accepted Jesus Christ, but that does not mean you will have it at easy, no the devil will fight you and try to take away the grace from you. The thing is when you accepted Jesus Christ you declared war with the devil, you became his main enemy because you are a threat to him and his kingdom.

Everyone that has a vision receives attacks around him/her, meaning vision brings attacks. The devil won't waste his power and time on something he does not see as a threat, that's why as a Christian you will come across mountains and seas oftentimes. Vision gives birth to a mission, there cannot be a mission without a vision, and these two work together.

Your vision as a Christian is to enter heaven therefore you must have a mission that will help you, take you to your vision which is heaven. This means without a mission the vision cannot come to pass. There are two things or qualities that a Christian must have to put into action every day of his/her life in order to reach heaven, namely **faithfulness** and **righteousness.**

Faithfulness

Faithfulness means being loyal and adhering firmly to one person or cause. As a Christian, you made a covenant to God and Jesus Christ that you will serve them alone for the rest of your earthly life, and they require you to remain faithful to them, it is your duty to be loyal to God looking that at the end you will be rewarded.

Look at the life of Jesus Christ, Jesus knew what He was coming to do here on earth (his vision) and that was to die on the cross for the whole world and to accomplish that He knew what he had to do (his mission). Christ knew that he had to suffer, to be persecuted and tormented.

That's why he persevered and endured through it all, even when it was not easy, but because he was looking at the victory ahead, he did not give up or complained but he remained faithful to the end, he was loyal to God to the point where it was very hard for him he ended up praying a prayer that says "not my will be done but let the will of God be done."

He only wanted to please God his father, the highest motive to serve God is the desire to please him. So you need to hold fast to this salvation looking at the reward that awaits you, the crown of glory that you will receive. Yes, you will come across difficulty to appoint where you feel like giving up but if your vision is heaven you will carry the cross and fight until the end, even when you are tempted to be unfaithful the vision you carry will help you to overcome that temptation and maintain the position of your heart with God, remember blessed are the pure in heart for they shall see the kingdom of God.

Righteousness

A Christian is a follower of Christ,
Christ was righteous so as a follower of
Christ you are required to display the
same character of Christ. If Christ was
righteous you must also be righteous
so you can be able to go where Christ is
and that is heaven. Christianity does
not just end at accepting Christ only,
but after receiving him you must live in
a way that will protect the grace you
have received of entering heaven,
receiving salvation is the first step that
qualifies you to get to know God.
Christianity is a lifestyle, not a religion,
it is not something we only observe on
Sunday or special occasions, but it is

the way we live every day of our lives on this earth, imitating Christ.

Romans 12:1

And so, dear brothers and sisters, I plead with you to give your bodies to God because of all he has done for you. Let them be a living and holy sacrifice- the kind he will find acceptable. This is truly the way to worship him.

You must live a righteous life offering your body as a living sacrifice, you must not defile yourself with things of this world but be blameless so when the day of the lord comes he must find you without any sin. Keep your heart clean and free from sin, let the Holy Spirit be the one that rules in your heart, let your heart be free and be in the character of Christ and the power of God shall work in you to the glory of God The grace of our Lord Jesus, the love of God and the sweet fellowship of the holy spirit be with you... AMEN.